IN CUSTODY
WOMEN IN TIHAR

ISBN: 978-81-7436-538-5

Published in India by
Roli Books in arrangement with
Roli & Janssen BV, The Netherlands
M-75, Greater Kailash-II Market,
New Delhi 110 048, India.
Phone: ++91-11-4068 2000
Fax: ++91-11-29217185
Email: info@rolibooks.com;
Website: rolibooks.com

Editor: Dipali Singh
Design: Supriya Saran
Production: Rajiv Kumar & Naresh Nigam

Printed and bound at
Ajanta Offset & Packagings Limited

IN CUSTODY
WOMEN IN TIHAR

Photographs: Renuka Puri

Text: Amba Batra Bakshi

Lustre Press
Roli Books

A courtyard within the ward where inmates dry their clothes and spend free time in the afternoon.

4
3

CONTENTS

Left: The matron at the main entrance

Taking pictures within the confines of Tihar was a difficult task. So was depicting the shades of black and white that I went to capture, only to find different colours within the inmates' lives. I was very apprehensive on my first visit to the country's largest jail, to meet the women inmates there. I expected it to be a pathetic life of women held captive, trusting my knowledge garnered from watching Bollywood films all my life. But the Jail was different. No living behind bars or dark rooms, but rather, a community living, loud chatter, joking around, dancing, agony aunts, mothers, sisters and friends. The jail is a dark place, no doubt, but not really!

Watching women move about freely in groups, albeit in a restricted space, was a surprise for me. At first, I was both excited and depressed, before I reminded myself that I was a photographer who had to look at that world only through my lens. Observing the space and its inhabitants was interesting: some were chatting, some drinking evening tea, some playing with their little ones, while some were busy at the busiest spot – the beauty parlour – giving and taking beauty care. The responses I got were also varied. While many were fascinated by the camera that always accompanied me, there were others who disliked me, thinking that I was using them to mint money. There were still others who thought I was a police spy, in spite of my protests that I was only a photo journalist.

This enriching journey would not have been possible without the support of a few. Here I would like to mention my husband Avinash and son Aakash, for understanding me and the reason for my absence during holidays and festivals. My editor in chief, Shekhar Gupta, for the support and freedom that he gave me. I also thank the Tihar Jail authorities, for allowing us a unique glimpse into the other side of the prison.

Renuka Puri

Facing page: An adult literacy programme, philosophical messages on walls and reading at leisure are a few measures encouraged to transform inmates.

I spent over a year visiting the women's jail at Tihar to complete my research on this book. I met women from different social and cultural backgrounds; ate meals with them, watched television and even got a pedicure by one of the inmates at the prison's beauty parlour! There was something unnervingly comfortable about the set-up inside and I would find myself constantly thinking if all prisons in the world were as deceptive from the outside. But of course, none of these things can take away the miseries of a life in confinement; they only better its quality by a few degrees.

Some women inmates confessed that they lived happier lives within the jail than they did outside. They had shelter and food, which in itself is a luxury for many, but many of them also had stories of desolation, of the pain of being away from loved ones, the slow judicial system and the overcrowded barracks. Not one woman confessed to her crime. They all seemed to be happily engrossed in adult literacy classes, candle making, crèche management and beauty parlour courses. The facilities were provided by the authorities but the effort made by the women to change, grow and rehabilitate themselves needs to be applauded. I take this opportunity to salute these women, for taking the initiative to bring change in their lives even as they fight their cases in court and live in confinement.

The names in this book have been changed in many cases to protect identity. All statistics relate to the year 2003-2004.

I would like to thank my parents Tania and Arjun Batra for being my best critics and my husband Farid Bakshi for his love and belief. I would also like to thank my former editor Shekhar Gupta, editor in chief, the Indian Express for giving us the permission to work on this project.

Amba Batra Bakshi

Facing page: Before her release, seventy-year-old Sona Devi (left) was the eldest woman inmate at Tihar, sentenced for dowry charges.

Inmates sell candles they have made as a part of prison activities to other inmates before festivals.

INTRODUCTION

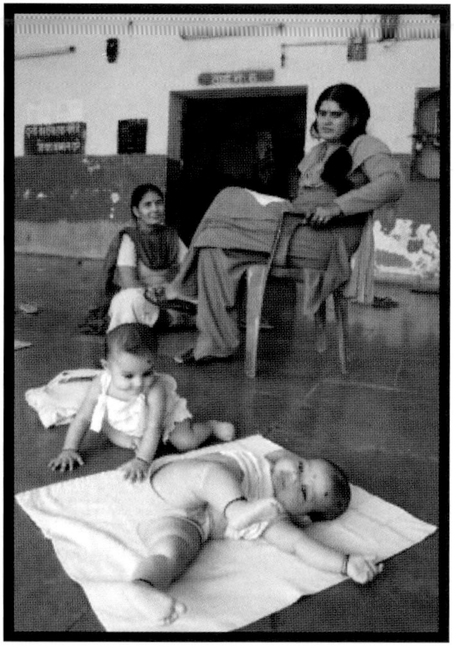

Guiltless but born in captivity, these babies play while the matron (seated) and an inmate oversees them. Inside the jail, mothers are provided with food, medical and day-care for their children. The mothers of these two babies did not want to be photographed.

A slow climb over the Janakpuri flyover in West Delhi, gives a visitor the first glimpse of the fortress that is Tihar Jail. Surrounded by lofty eucalyptus trees, barbed-wire fencing and circular watch bays at every few metres, it is the largest prison in South Asia. Once you enter the pale pink complex through the guarded gate, there are only a handful features, such as the steel gate and high wall, to convince you that this is a penitentiary. In more recent years, the jail has acquired fame for being one of the leading reformist prisons in this part of the world, with its innovative programmes for rehabilitation of prisoners.

Sprawled over 400 acres, the prison has the capacity to house 4,000 inmates, but at the time of our visit, it had as many as 13,781 inmates packed in the seven jails on its campus. Jail Number Six, which was opened exclusively for women in the year 2000, houses 600 inmates, when its total capacity is for only 400.

Eighty per cent of the women at Tihar are under-trials. Of those convicted, sixty women are serving life sentences. No one at the women's jail has received the death sentence yet. The common crimes here are dowry-related crimes, murder, drug trafficking, prostitution and financial crimes.

Jail Number Six is the first in the row of Tihar's seven jails. A narrow road with high concrete walls on either side leads to an enormous steel gate, which is bolted and guarded on both sides. It is opened only twice a day; first to let the van with under-trial inmates depart for city courts in the morning and again, when they are brought back in the evening.

It is the world behind these steel gates that reveals stories of desolation and pain, but also of hope. Once inside the gates, the jail transforms into a place that is completely the opposite of what it projects from the outside. Eight wards are situated in cottage-like houses with red roofs and large courtyards, set in a large circular design that resembles a resort. Each ward has individual cells and barracks where the inmates stay. Lush green lawns and trimmed hedges line the buildings. The pavements are clean, the floors are sparkling and an antiseptic smell is omnipresent. In the distance, spirals of smoke shoot up to the sky, signalling that lunch is being prepared.

There are no prisoners in uniform and no barbed-wire fencing or iron bars. Nothing about the place feels like a jail. It is just the iron grills outside every cell, which upon a closer look, give the secret away.

No woman in Tihar confesses to her crime. The objective of telling their stories here is not to sympathize with or question their cases. Nor are these stories about praising the efforts being made by the prison in assisting the inmates with their reform process. Instead, these are mere observations of how women endure their time spent at the jail, survive through their darkest hours, and find a deep-rooted strength, both individually and collectively.

While every cell has a TV (to avoid fighting among the inmates), the women confessed that their favourite pastime remains chatting with each other.

Chapter 1 **MURDER FOR DOWRY**

Facing page: Eighty per cent of the women here are under-trials. The most common crimes committed by them are dowry related.

In the courtyard of Ward Number Seven, about thirty women in faded saris huddle in small groups to sun their hunched backs. The women are released from their cold cells for a few hours every winter afternoon to play dice games and discuss trivia. The average age of women in this ward is sixty and they are either convicts or are under-trials for dowry-related crimes, earning their section the sobriquets of 'Saas-bahu' ('Mothers-in-law, Daughter-in-law') Ward.

Kala Bai sits alone, enjoying the breeze caressing her creased face. Every now and then she stares at her wrist. As I approach her, she stretches her arm out lazily for me to inspect. The watch shows ten minutes to twelve o' clock – but the time on Kala Bai's wrist never changes, for the watch is actually a tattoo engraved on her skin. She says she cannot remember how young she was when her father had the outline tattooed on her wrist as a gift and did not understand its relevance until today, when time stands still for her.

Kala Bai is serving a life-term for poisoning her daughter-in-law and three other male members of her family are also serving the same

The world behind the steel gates tells stories of desolation, pain and hope.

sentence for the murder. Kala Bai's life sentence, which stretches to twenty years, at best can be cut down to fourteen, and would make her ninety-years-old when her day of freedom comes. She knows that with her frail health, she is unlikely to see the outside world again.

Dressed in a printed cotton sari with her *pallu* over her head and seemingly resigned to her fate, this seventy-five-year-old lady never admits to her crime.

The latest figures indicate that the number of women coming into the prison for dowry death cases is on a steep rise. The percentage of men

Inside, the jail is transformed into a place that is quite the opposite of what it projects from the outside.

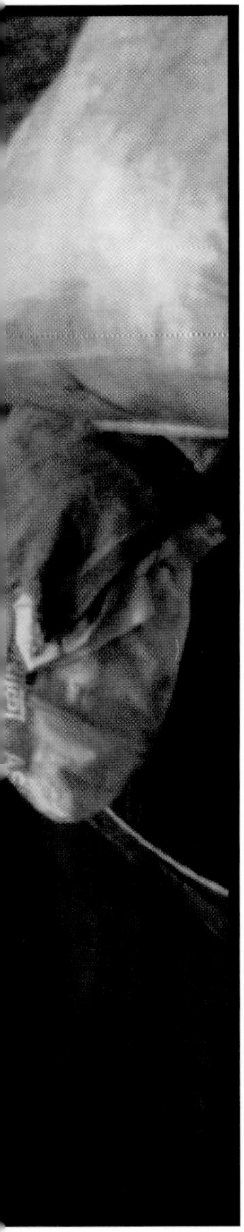

The overcrowded barracks look spacious in the day-time as a few inmates take a nap.

imprisoned for dowry-related crimes is 2.5 per cent of the total of male under-trials whereas the cases are a high 19 per cent of the total for women under-trials. Most women are from rural areas. Jail authorities also say that they mostly come from the lower middle class, though these crimes are committed by women of other sections of society, very few of those cases are reported as middle- and upper-class families tend to protect the offender from the social stigma of committing a crime. A very small percentage of women from these families are convicted and the under-trials usually serve only half the minimum sentence.

Housing over seventy women in six barracks, Ward Number Seven is a specially created ward for women who are jailed for dowry-related crimes. With room for only four hundred inmates, the jail is overcrowded as it accommodates more than six hundred women.

Sixty-four year-old Angoori moves away from her circle of friends towards us, and waits patiently for her turn to talk to us. Sitting on her haunches in a red *ghagra* (skirt), with silver ornaments adorning her hair, she shifts her body weight from one thigh to another with timely precision. Angoori and her husband are in jail for instigating their daughter-in-law to kill herself after a few months of marriage to their son. They belong to a remote village in Rajasthan.

At the time of conviction, it was stated that Angoori had demanded a gold chain from her daughter-in-law, which was not given to her. She denies the allegations as her eyes fill up with tears. To cheer her up, a few women rush into their cells and bring out packets of *namkeen* (savoury snacks) and biscuits which they are allowed to purchase from the 'Dry' and 'Wet' canteens at the prison. 'They sell lipstick, nail polish and Anne French cream too,' giggles Ram Rati, an under-trial for the same type of crime as Angoori, tugging another inmate at the waist. A few of them deviate from the topic of crime and joke about the products and facilities available to

Surrounded by lofty eucalyptus trees, the prison campus looks like a fort from the outside. It has high walls, barbed wire fencing and circular watch bays at every few meters. Spread over 400 acres, Tihar is the largest prison in Southeast Asia.

From Left to Right:

Chores such as ironing clothes, allow the women to 'earn' while in jail. In exchange for their work, they get coupons instead of money, with which they can shop at the dry/wet canteens.

Twice a day (10:00 am – 1:00 pm and 4:00 – 6:00 pm), the expanses of the jail courtyard are teeming with women and the laughter of children allowed to play outside.

Cooking for nearly 700 prisoners, three times a day, is the biggest 'job' inside the jail. While it is compulsory for convicts to work in the kitchen, under trials can volunteer in making the *langar*, as they call it.

them in the jail. 'We get handbags, *mehendi*, Boroplus, Ayur cream and bras too,' they cackle.

And then, from the outer boundary of the circle comes a comment in a shrill voice, 'They won't admit it, but the black hair dye sells the most, courtesy us old women!' And the courtyard erupts with their laughter.

The inmates at the jail get to buy these items with their earnings from the number of jobs they do on the premises. While the work is voluntary for the under-trials, it is mandatory for those convicted, a part of their sentence. Their earnings are accumulated and credited on a smart card with which they can buy items from the canteens. Products made by the inmates are also sold in the outside world.

A variety of vocational courses such as weaving, stitching, *agarbatti* (incense-stick) making, crèche management and beauty treatment are on offer for the inmates to choose from, as well as Vipassana and other meditation courses, such as the Art of Living course. The men's jail has a few more choices, with a bakery, weaving centre, oil-extracting section, a paper factory and a stitching and tailoring unit on the premises. Over the years, these centres have gained a lot of popularity, with Tihar Jail's (known as 'TJ's') confectionery becoming a favourite brand not only for the inmates but for the people of Delhi. Theatre is another popular option in prison with inmates performing plays for the public a few times in a year.

Under-trial workers are paid daily wages that have been categorized into three different sections: Rs 10 for trainees, Rs 12 for semi-skilled inmates and Rs 16 for skilled workers. However, in this ward, very few women have opted for work due to their age.

Glasses of steaming tea arrive again for the women talking to us just a few minutes before they return to their cells, and the others get ready for the night shift at the jail's kitchen. And so our time with these women draws to a close.

There are two canteens at Tihar. A 'Dry' canteen and 'Wet' canteen. While the dry canteen sells provisions such as namkeens, biscuits, lipstick, nail polish, hair dye, mehendi, creams, bra's and other basic things, the wet canteen provides tea and fresh snacks.

The jail makes no special arrangements for any religion, however, inmates are allowed to gather and pray. Women pray everyday in the prison, and larger gatherings are held on festivals with special food made on Diwali, Id and Christmas.

There are no religious segregations inside the jail. In fact, there is mutual respect for all religions; seen here is a Muslim woman (extreme left) praying alongside Hindu women.

Chapter 2 **A POSITIVE ATTITUDE**

There are few women who would say that their time spent in jail has not been bad. And even fewer would openly and comfortably admit that theirs has been a positive experience. But Mary D'Souza (name changed), a literate, middle-class businesswoman, is an inmate who says she has not disliked life in prison.

Completing nearly ten years in and out of the confines of Tihar, Mary, at forty-eight, is still fighting many charges of cheating, bouncing of cheques and other financial crimes involving international money transactions that have been made against her. And yet, she candidly admits to truly enjoying her time in jail. 'I woke up this morning and started wondering about what I should wear today. I need to put away my summer clothes and take out my winter ones. Just things I would do on an ordinary day if I were at home. I know if I were to tell someone that I feel at home in jail they would think I am crazy,' she says, refusing to be photographed.

Mary shares the floor space in jail with the rest of the inmates. Though she belongs to the minority of literate people in the prison, this

Facing page: The jail's holistic environment has given a new lease of life to many. This woman, known as the 'tough man' among inmates, not only tinkers around fixing bulbs etc., but also looks after the gardens.

No one at the women's jail has received the death sentence. Crimes broadly include, murder, drug trafficking, prostitution and financial crimes. Wives of underworld dons from Mumbai are also serving time here.

does not give her any extra civil liberties.

Dressed on the day of our meeting in a pair of blue trousers and a beige cardigan, she says that her life, even with all her troubles, seems fine: 'Human nature can really surprise you and I have learnt so much about myself here. Out here, you are at the bottom and there is no lower place to go.'

And while she consciously does all she can to adjust herself to this world, it's the craving to see her children that makes her efforts weak sometimes. 'My eldest daughter has just written to me from the US and

her first baby is due this Christmas. When I miss my children, I sit down and make cards for all of them out of cartoon strips from old newspapers.' She goes on to explain how she has tried to help her family battle the stigma of her being in prison in her own way: 'I have told them it is nothing to be embarrassed about and to just inform those who ask why I am in jail, that I am a state guest,' she laughs.

It is this incredible ability see the humorous side of almost every situation, laugh at herself and maintain an enviable self-confidence that makes her a popular woman at the jail. Most of the inmates find her

The jail has many under trial prisoners, some of them quite young, who are here on various criminal charges. They wait silently for their verdict.

approachable, and since only five per cent of all the women in the jail are literate, Mary is often requested to write letters and bail applications for them.

Even the jail authorities have decided to put her abilities to better use. So when a caretaker was required to look after three mentally handicapped inmates, Mary was an obvious choice. 'She is an intelligent woman and more than that, she is very responsible and is always willing to help. She asked us for two girls to help her look after the mentally ill inmates. We agreed to do so and their progress has been very good,' said an official at the jail. And so, in her small way, Mary is making her contribution towards a better life in prison – for others and herself.

Inmates can choose from are a number of vocational courses such as weaving, stitching, *agarbatti* (incense) making, crèche management, and beauty parlour course amongst others.

Chapter 3 **GROWING OLD IN PRISON** SONA DEVI MANGE RAM

The oldest woman inmate at Tihar is Sona Devi Mange Ram. The seventy-six year old is serving a seven-year sentence in a dowry-related crime. She has not even completed a quarter of her sentence, but is suffering from tuberculosis and is mostly kept in the jail's medical ward. Her feeble body and age do not allow her to remember clearly how she spent her life beyond the iron bars of Tihar, which is her world now.

She has been given an early reprieve from imprisonment and now awaits the release of her husband and son, who are also serving time in the same case.

It is difficult growing old in confinement, she says. She pats her frail hand on the hard mattress and asks me to sit at her side for a chat. In the medical room, Sona Devi is a favourite among all the younger women. They call her *Amma* (mother) with affection, and often exchange stories, taking advice from her on matters ranging from love affairs to bringing up children, and asking her to give them grandmother remedies that have been passed down for generations.

Facing page: An elderly woman sits outside the ward for dowry cases and sifts through personal papers.

Inmates playing their own version of dice games. They are permitted to spend the evening time, before and after dinner, together.

Doing odd-chores inside the prison.

But Sona Devi confesses that she is more popular for her wit and sense of humour, the latest Bollywood dances, which she likes to perform, and a very sharp tongue. Perched on the iron hospital bed in the centre of the medical room, Sona Devi fiddles with her silver toe-rings as she declares: 'I have never tried to befriend most of these women.' She enjoys being a difficult-to-please guest at the prison and ensures that the prison staffers fuss over her. They bring her special *dalia* (porridge) for breakfast, the way she likes it, which she believes will alleviate her low blood pressure to some extent. Sometimes, when the care and medical attention available at the in-house hospital seems insufficient for her, arrangements

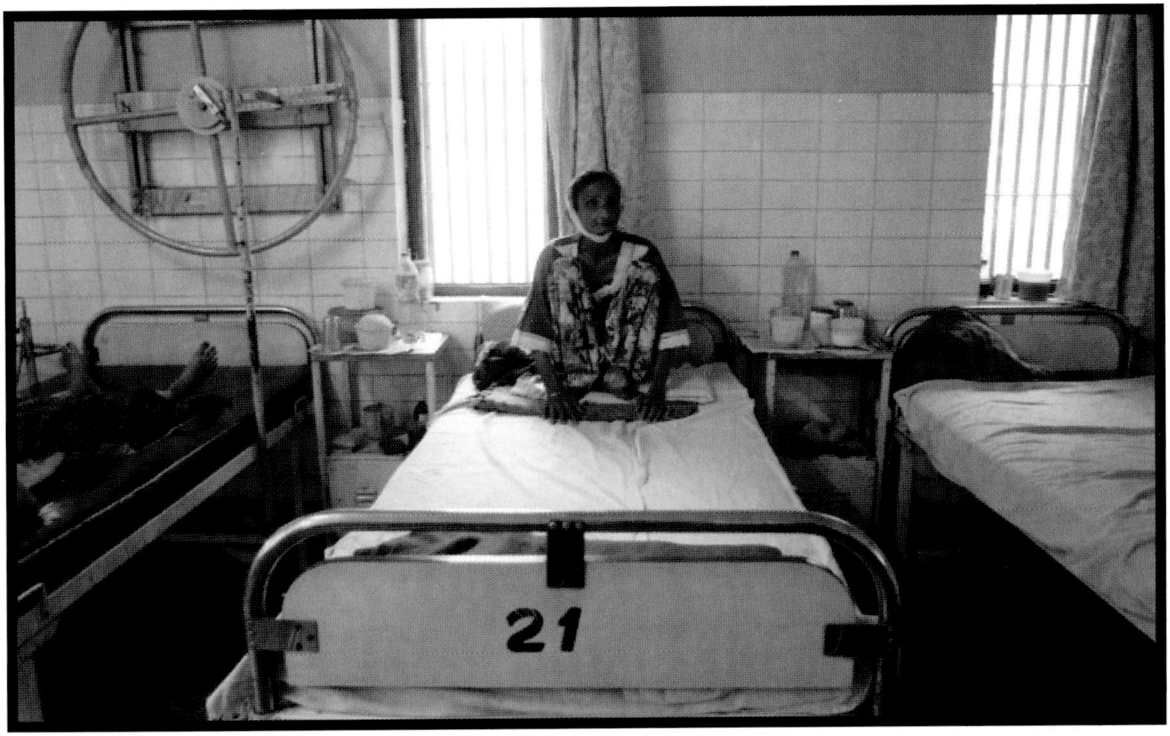

Sona Devi Mange Ram perched up on her hospital bed.

are made at hospitals in the city, and she is shifted for a few days. Sona Devi believes she receives medical attention that is superior to what she and her family would have been able to afford outside the jail.

Unlike the other women, Sona Devi does not find it necessary to proclaim to everyone that she is innocent and that she was framed for a crime she never committed. She is resigned to her fate. Instead of lending an ear to the details of others' cases, or presenting her own, she is quick to scold them for always desiring a public hearing.

As lunchtime now approaches, her eyes shift to the large clock placed at the entrance of the medical room. And before Sona Devi can

Solitary moments for the elderly inmates, many of whom feel they will not see the outside world again.

utter a word in complaint, her *thali* (plate) with *dal* (lentils) and *roti* (bread) is placed in front of her. She immediately soaks three rotis in the bowl of dal and puts them aside because she needs the rotis to become softer to enable her to chew them. The authorities have also added half a kilogram of milk and eggs to supplement her diet, but Sona Devi wishes to be provided with more fruit. She says, 'Winter is about to set in and I feel like eating oranges. I also wish for cups of hot tea every few hours. But the tea here is no better than dishwater.'

Deviating from her complaints about the food at the jail, she asks the women to assemble around her as she narrates stories of her younger days. She tells them about the endless hours she could spend washing

clothes and cleaning the house without getting tired. But when the women laugh at her and express doubts that she had so much stamina, Sona Devi leaps up from her bed and heads for the radio. She raises the volume as the jockey announces a foot-tapping Punjabi number. 'It's the only way they will believe that I had the stamina of a horse,' she says, and musters up a few moves. With the room now filled with loud beats of the *dhol* (drums), the other women leave their hospital beds and decide to hold a small competition. Sona Devi finds the offer hard to resist, and gets ready to put her best foot forward. And she beats all the younger women with the dexterity of her steps, showing that age and adversity need not dampen the human spirit…

Many women who have been in the jail for a long time admit that they have given up hope of ever getting out. Some even prefer it; with medical attention and other facilities, it is more secure than their life outside.

Inmates personalise their private spaces in jail.

Chapter 4 **CHILDREN AT TIHAR**

The first rain of the monsoon is pelting down and the children at Tihar are full of excitement. They wiggle out of their mothers' tight grips, and from the cots in the crèche, to play in the rain.

Two-year-old Gautam loves eating green grapes. Now dry, he sits in his mother's cell and picks the fruit out of a yellow polythene bag, cherishing each one. While children at Tihar are given fruit once a day, special fruit, such as these grapes, has been brought for Gautam by his relatives this morning.

Gautam is among the forty-five children who live with their mothers at Tihar. While some are born here, some come in when they are only a few months old, but all have to leave as soon as they turn five.

Collaboration with an NGO ensures that they are sent to a boarding school. Initially, the programme found some resistance, but after the first batch of children came back with wonderful stories about the school, more and more mothers agreed to send their children there.

Mamta, twenty-five, has just sent her five-year-old daughter Meenakshi away to the boarding school that is run at the outskirts

Facing page: Oblivious to their unusual confinement, the children at Tihar enjoy a normal childhood till they are old enough to understand the peculiarity of their predicament

The afternoon crèche at the jail is managed by Navjyoti, an NGO run by Kiran Bedi, former Director General of the prison. The morning crèche is run by other NGOs.

वार्ड नं:5

Breakfast comprises of fruit, milk, a piece of rusk and *dalia*. In the afternoon, the lunch menu varies from *khichri* to *channas* and *kheer*.

of Delhi. 'They give them good food and keep them very clean,' she says. 'They also teach them to read and write in English,' says Mamta. Convicted for killing her ex-husband, Mamta has already been in prison for the last five years. She was pregnant when she came into jail, and delivered Meenakshi here. Like all pregnant women in jail, Mamta was put on a more nutritious diet that included fruit and a glass of milk.

While the maximum number of women who share the space in each cell is three, up to twenty-five women sleep in a hall in the barracks. A special ward has been assigned to mothers who have their children with them, but the only additional facility they are given is an extra mattress

A special ward has been assigned to mothers with children.

for the child. The children must share the space with their mothers and do not have separate accomodation.

Children who are under the age of five can be left at a crèche for the entire day while their mothers are at work. Started in 1991, the crèche is run by two NGOs, one in the morning shift and the other in the afternoon. The Mahila Pratiraksha Mandal runs the morning crèche, where the children are given a breakfast of a fruit, milk, a piece of rusk and *dalia* (porridge). In the afternoon, the lunch menu varies from *khichri* (lentils and rice) to *channas* (chickpeas) and *kheer* (pudding of milk and rice). Voluntary organizations and diplomats often donate stuffed toys, swings and clothing. The afternoon crèche has most of its funding from

Children spend five years in the crèche that is inside the jail, and managed by Kiran Bedi's NGO Navjyoti. After that, a trust sponsors their admission to a boarding school.

the Royal Netherlands Embassy and the Royal Danish Embassy and is managed by Navjyoti, an NGO run by Kiran Bedi, former Director General of the prison. Here the children can sleep in the afternoons, the younger children in cots and the older ones in beds.

Two-year-old Peter is the only foreigner among the children at the crèche. Bouncing a deflated football, he has just been taught to say 'namaste' with his hands folded. He is a role model for the other children, who take a cue from him and stand up to salute us. Peter's mother, a Nigerian, is an under-trial. He has a twin brother, Paul, who is not permitted into the crèche, as he is HIV+ like his mother. Though Peter is fine, special care has to be taken with him too.

Nap time in the crèche.

Of the 590 women in jail currently, sixty have children. Sashi, thirty, who is convicted for murder, has delivered a baby girl just four days ago and still feels weak. She has no clothes for the baby, and has requested the officials to give her some; they promise to make the necessary arrangements. For most women whose husbands are also in prison, the children stay with the mother and are allowed to meet their fathers every Saturday.

The crèche has a dual purpose. Started in 1991, it provides a place for the children to be cared for and provides training to inmates on how to plan and manage a crèche.

Chapter 5 **THE BEAUTY PARLOUR**

A sharp white thread clenched tightly between her *paan*-stained teeth forms a diamond shape as it touches Meenu's upper brow covered in powder dust. The diamond formation closes in on the fine hair as Shaila Azhar pulls the thread back with slight force. The black, prickly, short strands of hair, which had grown like weeds around Meenu's pencil-thin eyebrow have been successfully pulled out for the brow to take a new arched shape.

The beauty parlour at Tihar's women's cell is more than a centre for leisurely indulgence. While the women can avail of most of the services that they could at parlours in the city of Delhi, the main intention of opening the beauty parlour at Tihar is to train inmates. Inmates receive a certificate once they have completed a six-month course and worked for a short time. The certificate does not mention that they are inmates at Tihar and is issued by an NGO. This is done to make it easier for the women to get work after they are released.

Facing page: An inmate enjoys a facial and a pedicure being performed by a fellow inmate who is training to be a beautician. The officer watches and waits for her turn.

Instead of whiling away her time in the prison, Shaila thought it would be beneficial to take up the beauty parlour course that the jail was

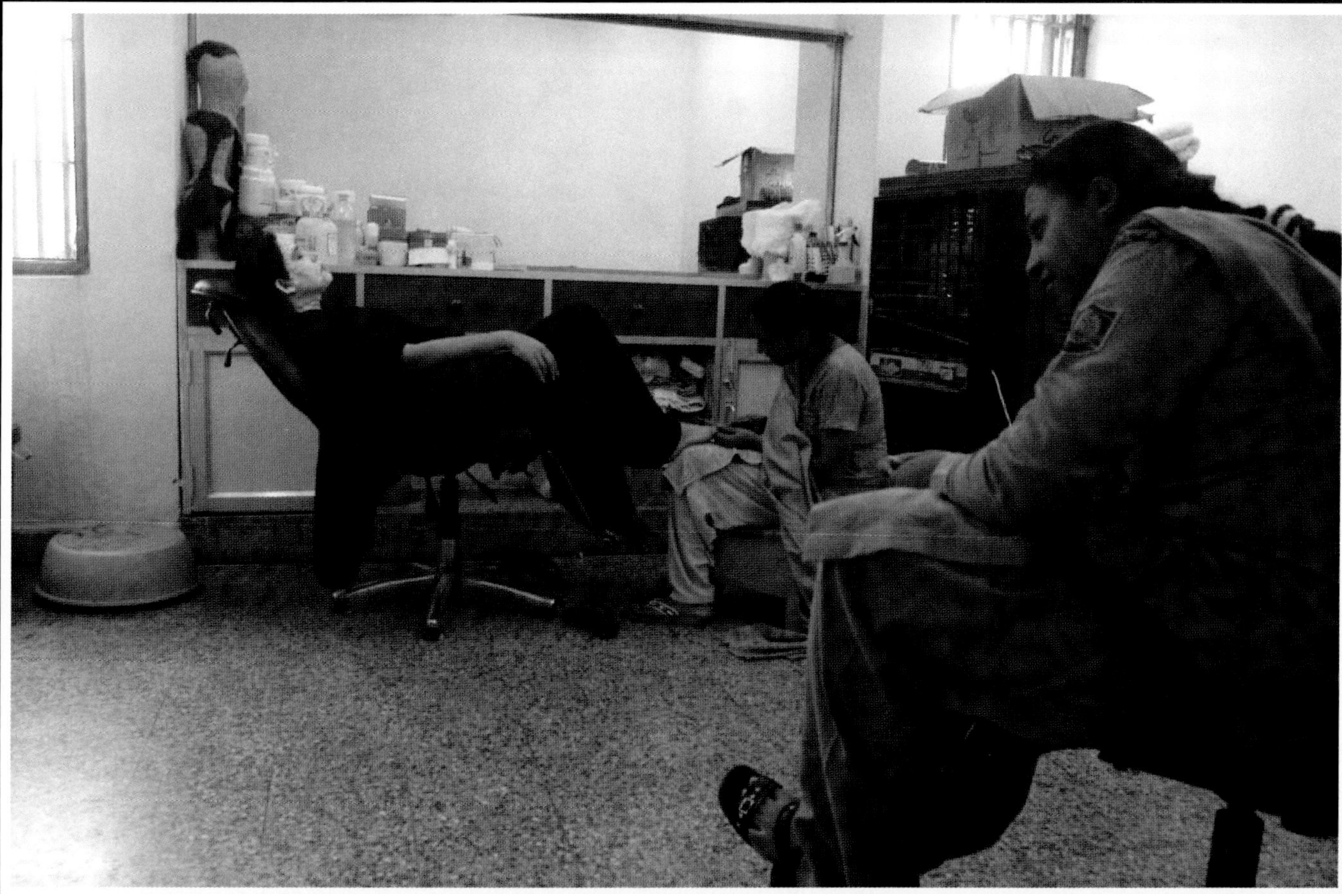

offering. Shaila is an under-trial for possessing a fake passport and has been incarcerated for four and a half years. 'One can order the shade of the latest hair colour and even request for a particular shade of nail polish. It is during festivals such as Diwali and Karva Chauth (fast for the well-being of husbands) that the parlour does maximum business. Last time we requested for the new Garnier Burgundy hair colour because we saw it was in vogue,' says Shaila, who is considered the best hairdresser in the jail. 'Every woman in the jail wanted her hair to be that colour. The women here are very beauty conscious. It does not matter to them that they are in jail. What matters more is to look good for themselves and for the other women,' says Shaila.

Tihar also offers inmates Bachelor of Arts, Master of Arts, certificate and diploma courses in subjects like tourism, management, computer education, and so on. In the men's jails, there are more centres for activity than at the women's cell with modules in pen-making, bookbinding, manure-making, screen-printing, envelope-making, tailoring and cutting and shoe-making. The men's jail also houses a bakery, a paper unit, a chemical unit, a carpentry unit, a weaving section and a tailoring section. These programmes were introduced with the aim of reforming prisoners and giving them additional skills when they return to a normal life outside the jail.

Applying *mehendi* (henna) during the festival seasons is also a favourite with the inmates, and the trainees at the parlour are taught how to make various designs. The art of applying mehendi is also a vocational option for many women once they are released. Santosh Shyam, serving a ten-year term under the NDPS Act, is a regular customer at the beauty parlour. 'I love coming here as it makes me feel good after I pamper myself. I like getting everything done from a facial to pedicures. It is not like the parlours outside but it's very nice. I like the nail paint colours here and like to apply them myself. On the days when I know that my

Inmates gather together to participate in the traditional Karva Chauth puja ceremony. Special food is prepared for them after they break their fast.

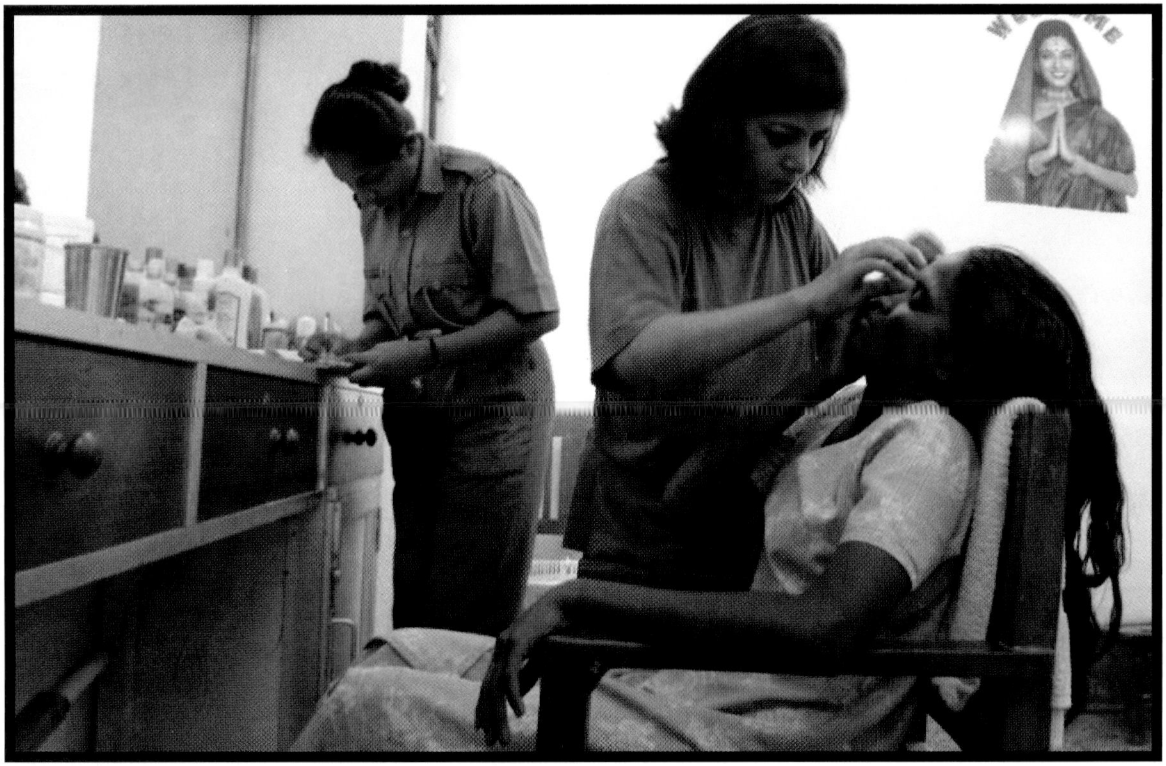

Shaila is considered the best beautician at the Jail.

children and husband are coming to meet me, I end up spending half the day here,' she says.

It is inside the four walls of the parlour, which resembles a classroom with equipment used for training lying on the tables, that the women tease each other, share stories about children and families and dissect the latest episodes of all the Ekta Kapoor soaps. 'We spend a lot of time here and this is when we forget we are inmates. We feel like a bunch of regular girls who are visiting the parlour. We chat about movies and other little things. It's amazing how quickly this small room can make you forget you are in jail,' says Shaila, unwittingly showing that it is the tiny pleasures in life that can lift a person out of the reality of any grim situation, however brief the respite may be.

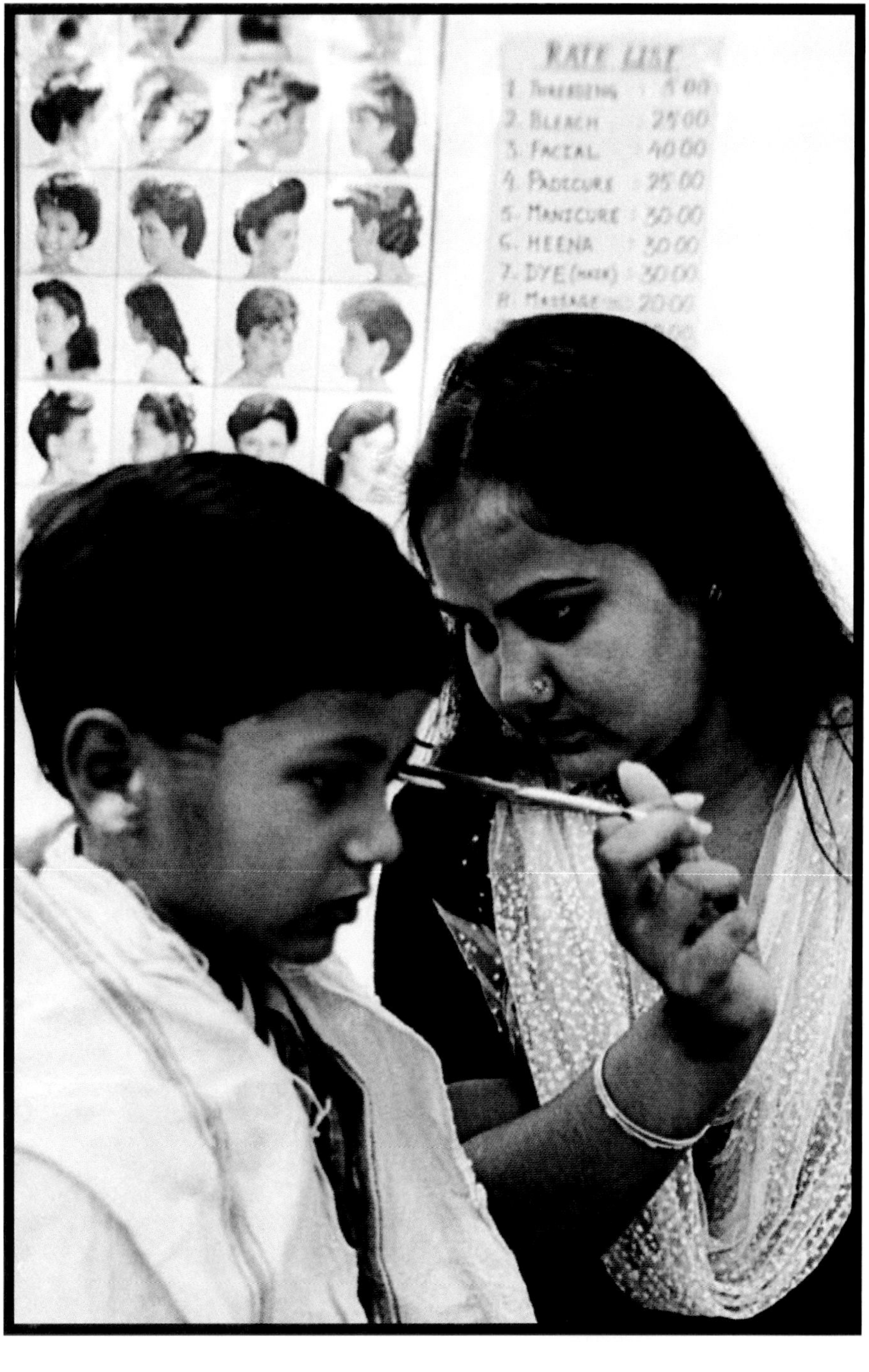

A mother cuts her child's hair.

8
7

The prison doubles up as a learning ground for children where bars and locks replace toys.

Chapter 6 JAILED ON FOREIGN GROUND

Few situations are harder than a life in confinement, except for spending that life-term in a jail on foreign soil. Sepiso Lubinday, a Zambian national, has experienced this misfortune. She speaks of the hardships in a foreign country, surrounded by alien people: 'The manners, the food and the habits of the people are difficult to adapt to. And it's the hardest when we see others receiving visitors, but no one comes to see us,' she says in broken English.

The forty-five-year-old was caught at New Delhi's Indira Gandhi International Airport by the Airport Authority for carrying drugs, and was handed over to the police. Under trial for possession of drugs under the Narcotic Drugs and Psychotropic Substances (NDPS) Act, she has already spent two and a half years at Tihar. She does not know how much longer the slow judicial system in India will take to decide her fate.

'I have three children of my own and three adopted orphans. I have to survive this for them and go back home as soon as I can,' says Sepiso.

She had come to India for shopping, like many other young women

Facing page: An African inmate and an Indian inmate go for a walk like regular friends.

Young European girls are in the jail under prostitution charges. Jail authorities say they are quick to fight with the local inmates and prefer to form their own groups.

Stella, a forty-four-year-old convict from Zambia has been here since 2002. She is in charge of the crèche and described by others as 'very friendly'.

A foreign inmate (above) plays with the children at the creche and another (right) shares her grievances with the superintendent.

from her country who were trying to cash-in on the mammoth demand for Indian goods back in their country.

Currently, nine other women from the African subcontinent are within the confines of Tihar. All of them have been arrested under the NDPS Act, but only two are serving their sentence while the others are under-trials. This is the only crime under which parole is not admissible.

However, to occupy herself until she can go back to her country,

Santosh (center) was the superintendent of the jail but has now left. The job wields authority and discipline, but the women in-charge are also lenient and at times, motherly.

Sepiso has put all her energies into teaching herself more about positive thinking, patience and perseverance. The books in the jail's library have helped her and she likes the collection that the prison has built up over time through donations and charity. Most of the books available at the library are in the fiction and best-seller categories, but Sepiso prefers the books on religion and self-help books on how to live in a better, more peaceful way.

Sepiso has picked up some words in Hindi and says, '*Bahut mirchi hai*?

(Is the food is very hot?).' Spicy Indian food has left her with an infected and damaged oesophagus: 'My voice has turned hoarse because I cannot stomach the fiery food. The food here is very different from what we eat at home. The spices may be nice once in a while, but when we have to eat them every day, our bodies cannot take it. On festive holidays like Christmas, however, we request the jail staff to make special food for us and they do.'

Gently scratching her frail hands, fingernails coated with chipped red nail paint, she admits that not all the other foreign inmates are very friendly. Many young girls from European countries come into the jail under prostitution charges, but they tend to keep to themselves. Jail authorities say that they are quick to fight with other inmates and keep their distance from both the Indian inmates and the jail authorities. They form their own groups and tend to stick together, as a way of ensuring their own safety.

Although one seldom hears of torture within the prison premises here, there are a few isolated incidents. The foreign inmates say that they feel targeted and even though the prison guards do them small favours, such as procuring food or getting their letters sent across to their families, the foreigners often find themselves being treated worse than the Indian inmates. They recall an incident about a year ago when the jail guards suspected a foreign inmate of possessing a mobile phone. When they interrogated her, the inmate denied it. But the guards did not believe her and searched her for it. When they found nothing, they allegedly stripped her naked and beat her up in front of six hundred inmates. When she still did not confess to having it, one of the guards put on a glove and looked for it inside her vagina, traumatizing her.

Foreign women incarcerated in Tihar come from various countries all over the world, each one far away from home, doing time in an alien land.

Dancing Queens. Despite all the pain and anguish that is a part of prison life, these girls show that a life in confinement cannot take away simple joys of a song and dance.

Chapter 7 **THE KITCHEN**

The favourite item on the menu at the women's cell is *kadhi*, a lightly spiced dish made of yoghurt and gram flour. The women love this dish and often request the kitchen staff for it. The morning shift at the kitchen begins at 6 a.m. with tea, followed by breakfast, lunch and after another round of tea, ends with dinner at 6 p.m. The night shift begins at 11 p.m. and ends at 6 a.m. While the women in the morning shift or *langar*, as it is more popularly known among the inmates, prepare meals for all the inmates at the women's cell, the night langar women prepare packed lunchboxes for inmates who have a date at the court the next day.

Other favourite dishes cooked at the women's cell kitchen are *kofta* (vegetable or meat balls) curry and *kheer*, a milk and rice pudding, which is made twice a week. 'These are two items that we get a lot of compliments and requests for,' says Shanti, an inmate who is in charge of the morning shift. Sitting on the ground and cutting onions that make tears roll down her face, encircling her yellow nose-pin, she admits that work in the kitchen comes naturally to her after years of having done the same chores

Facing page: The kitchen functions round-the-clock and caters to nearly 1,500 inmates daily.

Each inmates has a fixed chore in the kitchen to ensure efficiency and quality on a daily basis.

at home. She does not feel that her labour every day is forced on her as a compulsory duty.

Inside the grey-tiled kitchen, which is lined with giant pots and pans, the work for the day is well distributed. While three ladies begin kneading the dough, three others heat the *tava* (griddle) to cook the chapatis. Opposite them sits another small cluster of women who busily chop vegetables. The older inmates are usually assigned to do the packaging during the night shift. The women at the prison kitchen work seven days a week, but those on the night shift need not work on the nights before the day that the courts remain closed.

Strict hygiene is maintained in the kitchen where meals are cooked for all the prisoners, thrice a day.

On this particular day, when we visit the jail, Shanti and the other ladies form a tight circle to distribute the tasks needed to prepare a special breakfast for the children at the jail. After this, they will prepare *poori-sabzi* (fried bread and vegetables) for lunch.

Mukesh Manoj has been appointed as the night kitchen in-charge. She is serving time for the murder of her neighbour and has already completed five and a half years at the jail. Most of her mandatory work under conviction has been in the kitchen. While she does not mind her work, she misses the joy that came from cooking for her two sons.

'I miss my children telling me that they liked a particular dish I had

Seasonal vegetables are bought by the authorities and given to the inmates. Special requests are made at the time of festivals. Inmates can also give their suggestions at the prison panchayat.

prepared specially for them and requesting me to cook their other favourites. Here the cooking is routine and with such large numbers to cater to, there are often complaints about the food.' Mukesh earns her monthly wages from her work at the prison kitchen. She is paid Rs 480 a month, most of which she spends on buying toiletries such as toothpaste and hair oil, which are available at the prison's 'Dry' canteen.

Women wait in the courtyard for the prison panchayat to start.

A small television set and magazine cut outs make this cell very popular.

The inmates are only in charge of cooking, while the prison authorities procure all the provisions. Five chapatis are made for each person and pieces of onion are also served along with the food. Whatever is cooked goes through a daily chain of quality control checks, which include tasting samples by the superintendent, medical officers and other officers before being served to the inmates. These steps are taken for security reasons and underline the fact that life in the prison has to be regulated and controlled.

Chapter 8 AFFIRMING BONDS OF FRIENDSHIP

Geetanjali and Devika (names changed) knew little about the power of friendship until they met at Tihar. Both under-trials for murder, they struck a chord at their first meeting. Geetanjali, a eunuch, was apprehensive about how the jail staff and other inmates would treat her, but Devika who had been there a while longer, took it upon herself to make Geetanjali comfortable.

Though she had reservations about eunuchs before coming to prison, Devika found it easy to approach and befriend Geetanjali inside the confines of the prison. 'I usually ignored *hijras* (eunuchs) on the streets and at the most, interaction would be limited to handing them some money once in a while. I never really cared to know them better. And now I feel there is no difference between them and us,' says Devika, who firmly believes that true friendships are initiated and established in the strangest situations.

Facing page: Women draw immense strength from each other's friendships to survive within prison walls.

Geetanjali looks and sounds like a male, but prefers to be addressed as female. However, Devika insists on calling her '*Bhaiya*' (Brother). They live in cells next to each other in Ward Number One or the

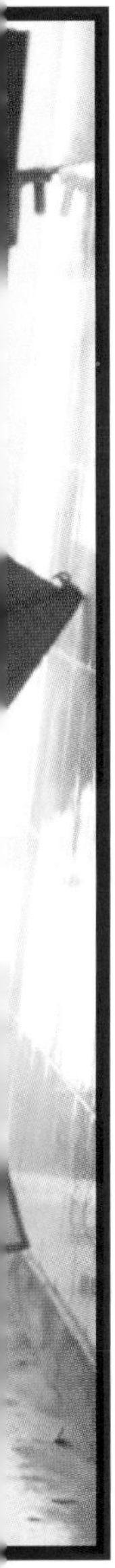

Difficult times can lead to strong friendships.

Tea and biscuit with friends

Vipassana (meditation) ward. This ward houses only under-trials and has a special room where Vipassana sessions are held once every two months.

Dressed in blue satin tie-and-dye pajamas and a white shirt, Geetanjali leads us to her cell. Graciously, she offers to share her lunch with us. Decorated with a large crayon drawing and posters of goddesses, the cell is very neat. Within the cell, a small television set is placed just outside the toilet space, which is separated by a cement partition. Tihar introduced cable television in 1994 for educational and recreational purposes and while a few black-and-white televisions are set up in the barracks, inmates are allowed to bring in their own portable sets.

Besides Vipassana classes, the two women keep themselves busy with voluntary work. Since they are under-trials, work in the jail is not

Women admire the *mehendi* they've applied for the festival of Karva Chauth (a day's fast for the well-being of husbands).

compulsory for them; however, the two feel it is a chance for them to learn a few new skills. So Geetanjali spends a few hours every day at the beauty parlour learning various useful skills, while Devika has taken up a few vocational courses such as weaving and crèche management so that she can get a job once she leaves the jail. The jail offers both adult and formal education, and has arrangements with study centres such as the Indira Gandhi National Open University (IGNOU) and National Open School. Computer education is also imparted to keen inmates and capsule courses for six months have been designed in order to benefit inmates who serve a short term. Devika had studied for the BA first-year examinations, but was too embarrassed to go to the examination centre with the mandatory police escort. But her story shows that there are possibilities in Tihar for those who wish to make use of them.

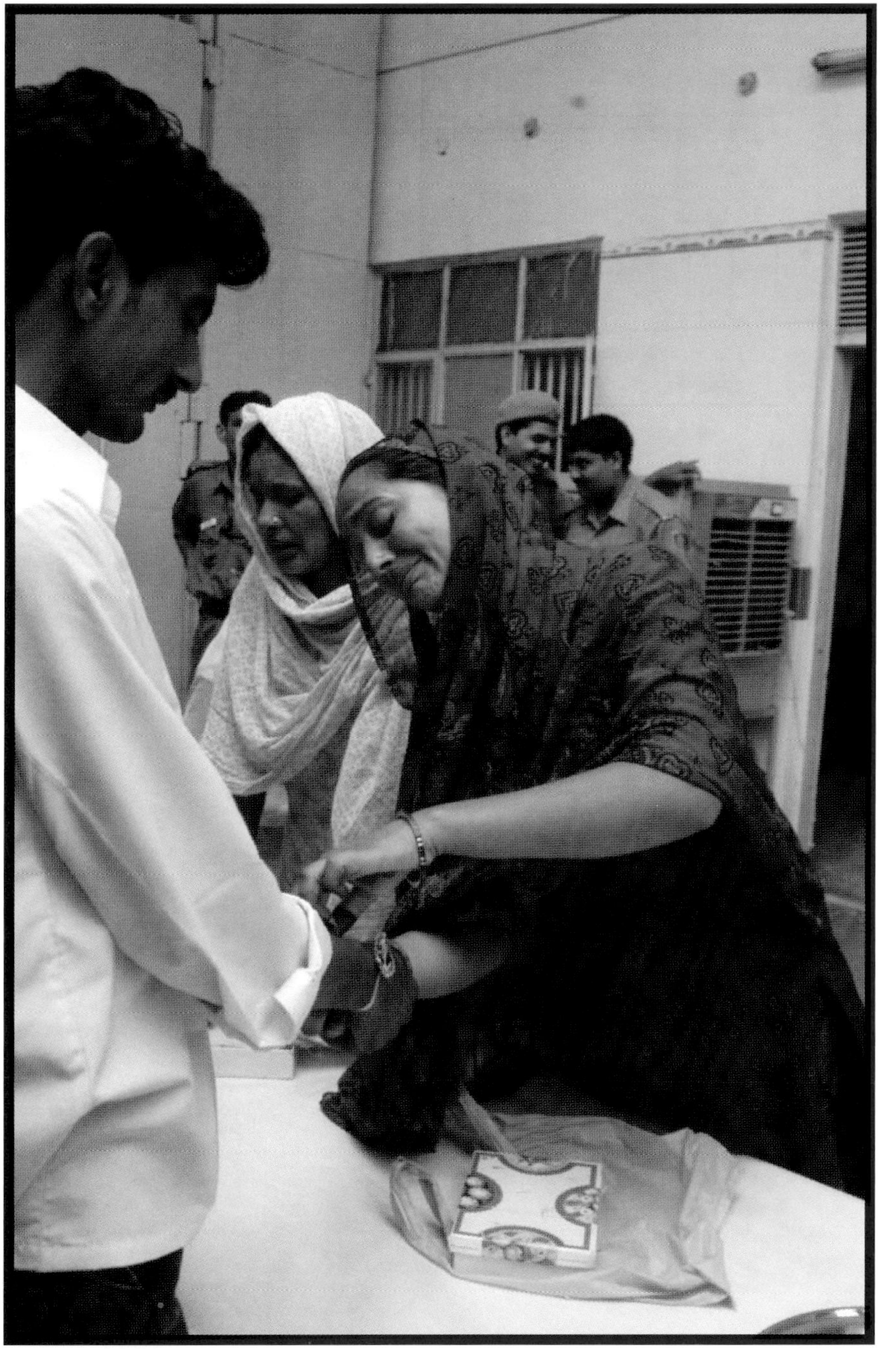

Raksha Bandhan. Festivals are a big occasion in the prison as inmates get to meet their families and celebrate.

Chapter 9 ANJALI: THE SOCIAL WELFARE OFFICER

Anjali is the first welfare officer at Jail Number Two. Her job entails listening to the problems of women inmates and providing them with emotional and psychological support. She is the first point of contact when a woman enters the jail.

Her office is strategically located in Ward Number Eight or Mulaiza, where the new entrants stay for the first three months. The Mulaiza is regarded as the most sensitive and protected area in the prison. It is here that the new inmates are shielded from the older prisoners, who could pose a threat to them in the form of sexual or psychological abuse.

'When they come in, they tell me certain things about themselves and about their cases. Most of them claim that they are innocent, but the few who do confess learn soon enough that they should not do so. It makes acceptance by other inmates harder. The inmates have to struggle for their own acceptance once inside the jail.'

Facing page: There are multiple security checks at the entrance of the prison as well as within. Here a group of young officers chat in the corridor.

Most of the six hundred women inmates in Tihar are under-trials and Anjali knows each one by name. Her popularity is a giveaway as the

While some officers mingle easily with the inmates, some like to keep their distance. Most officers are up to date with information about the inmates' cases and are willing to lend an ear to their grievances.

An officer signs in visitors during the *Mulaqaat* (visiting) timings.

women smile and greet her on her way down the tiled path from one ward to the other. 'Namaste, Didi' is what you hear in chorus every time you turn a corner or enter a ward with her.

Anjali has always made sure she has the time to ask the inmates how they are doing and spends more than the polite moment in inquiring about their likes and dislikes. On crossing an old lady she asks her, 'Why are you looking so glum and irritated today?' The lady replies that her children have not come to see her in a very long time. Anjali is quick

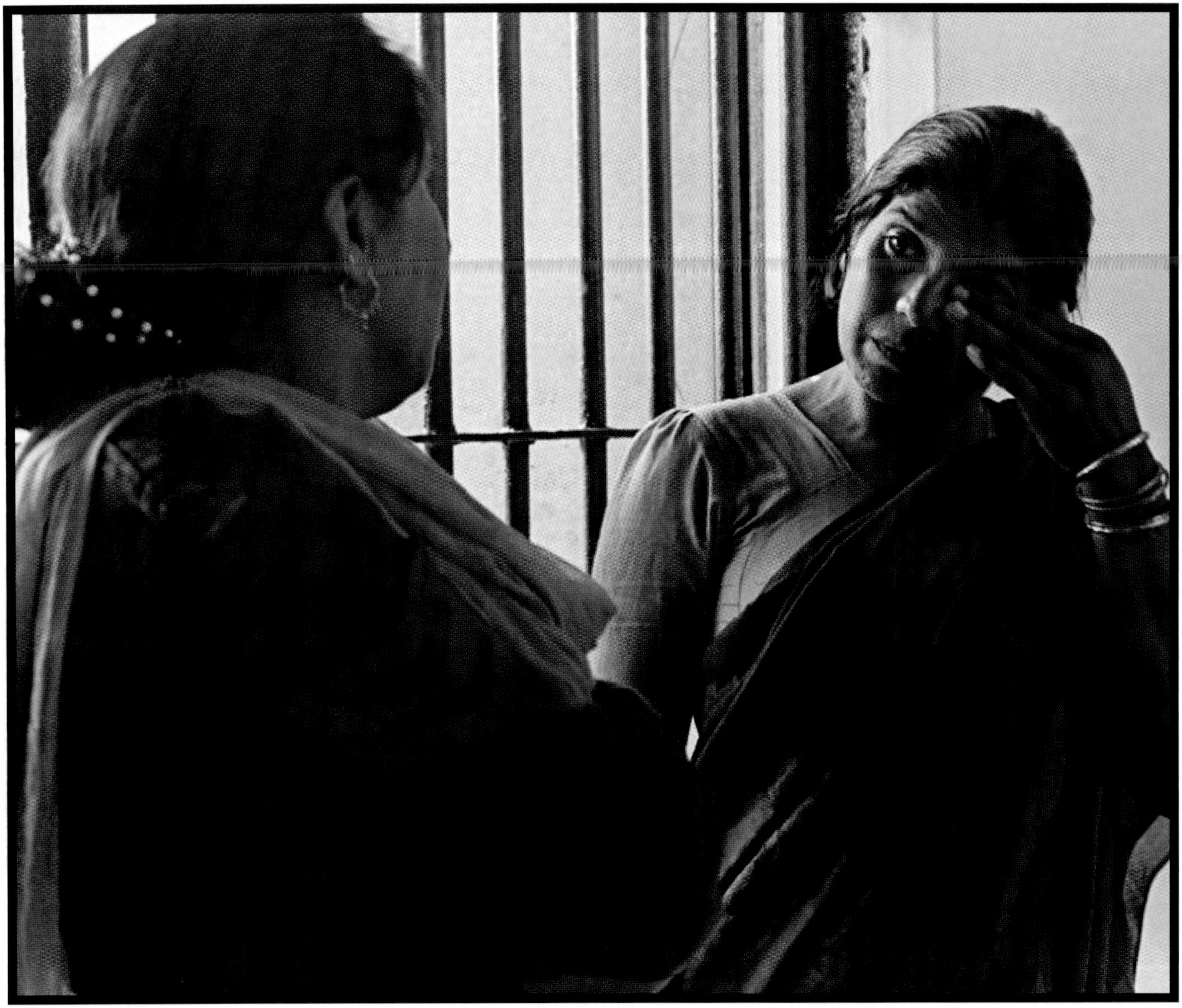

to cheer her up by telling her that she has ordered very fancy gold-rimmed glasses for her, which will be ready in a few days. 'I am here to act as a bridge between these women and their families. In a number of cases, the family deserts these women. In other cases, their families need to be contacted, so I have to locate them and establish contact.'

The inmates enjoy having her around as she shows them respect. 'Once an officer came into her office while I was discussing my problems with her. The officer asked me to get up and leave, but Didi objected and asked the officer to wait instead,' says Sonia, an inmate.

The posts of a welfare officer and a law officer were both created as a part of the proposed changes under the New Prison Act a few years ago. This was done in order to introduce modern concepts of prison management. However, Anjali feels that she is a complete antithesis of what the prison stands for. 'A prison is meant to take away all freedom from the individual brought in. And my job is exactly the opposite. I encourage them to talk, I push them towards change,' says Anjali.

Despite pressure from the family, who tried to dissuade her from taking the job, Anjali applied for it. Prior to this, she had been working as a social worker with a number of women's organizations. Extremely soft-spoken, she tells you that the inmates are like little children, who vie for her attention all the time.

'We have a few NGOs and trained psychiatrists who come here on a voluntary basis, but no one is there permanently. The women need counselling on a more regular basis. It is because of my consistency at work here that I have managed to develop a rapport with the inmates.' While walking from her office to other wards, she notices a four-year-old girl roaming about. She scolds her gently for not being at the crèche where all the other children are and asks her to run back quickly. And on watching her run, she pauses and sighs, 'I love my job, I sleep better at night now than I ever did.'

Officers wait for inmates to return to their cells to lock-up for the night.

This woman inmate pleads with her husband to let her keep both her children. Her husband had come from the men's jail to visit her on the occasion of Rakhi, pretending to be her brother. One child stays with the father, while the other stays in the women's jail with his mother.